Kay: Pam told me to shut up with politics & write a book!

So I did

Red

Yellow Dogs and Fruit Flies

Political Commentary of a Conservative Democrat

by

Rick Teal

authorHOUSE™

1663 LIBERTY DRIVE, SUITE 200
BLOOMINGTON, INDIANA 47403
(800) 839-8640
WWW.AUTHORHOUSE.COM

© 2004 Rick Teal
All Rights Reserved.

No part of this book may be reproduced, stored in a retrieval system, or transmitted by any means without the written permission of the author.

First published by AuthorHouse 08/05/04

ISBN: 1-4184-8656-6 (sc)

Printed in the United States of America
Bloomington, Indiana

This book is printed on acid-free paper.

Table of Contents

Forward ix

Chapter 1 Just Some Thoughts 1

Chapter #2 More on Terrorism 13

Chapter 3 The MEDIA 34

Chapter 4 The Economy 47

Chapter 5 What has happened to my Democratic Party 57

Chapter 6 Who am I to Talk? 69

Chapter 7 The Rest of the Story 84

Chapter 8 The Real of the Rest of the Story 93

Epilogue 101

A favorite expression of Southern Democrats of the 30's

"I'd sooner vote for a Yellow Dog as a Republican!"

Blaming Herbert Hoover and the Republican party for the Depression that had heaped such hard times on so many residents in the South of the 30's was a favorite pastime.

Historically, many Veteran's and son's of veterans of the Confederacy were still around in the early 30's.

Both easily understood reasons for mistrust of the Republican Party by Southern Democrats.

Forward

While writing this book, I found myself needing to preach, so I hope I have at least avoided it to some degree. I realize I have not been entirely successful. I have also resorted to Readers Cramp Relief at the beginning of each chapter, just a short break that will hopefully help set the mood for that chapter.

I also in each chapter try to divine at least one immutable truth that I have learned or been forced to accept at sometime during my life. Agree, or disagree, it is up to you entirely. Just bear in mind how fortunate we are in this country to be able to not only say what we want, but to also disagree with anyone we want, as long as we do it peacefully, or at least without violence. Keep in mind if you agree with me, you may be much more intelligent than you think and vice versa!

I have been a registered card carrying Democrat for most of my adult life. I was even what I considered liberal for much of my youth. But then I grew up and have been becoming more conservative ever since. Trouble is my democratic party has become more and more liberal until now it has completely ***Left*** (no pun intended) me behind. It has been this move to the left of my party, that has made me so cynical about our democracy and the political process. But regardless of that cynicism it is still the greatest form of government on earth, and as such it is our duty as citizens of the world to insure that every man, woman, and child on this old Earth at least has the right to experience and choose if they want a freely elected democratic form of government. We have to teach them that democracy represents a better way to govern themselves. We must continually take the moral high ground, regardless of the temptation to point our fingers and place blame, deserved or not.

Thanks for reading

Rick

Chapter 1
Just Some Thoughts

Reader's Cramp Relief: *While signing a receipt for my credit card, the clerk noticed that I had not signed the back of the card and refused to accept it until I signed it. When I asked her why she said it was necessary to compare the signatures in order to make sure that I was the person who was supposed to have it. Well I signed it for her and she scrutinized it closely and compared it to the receipt I had just signed also. As luck would have it they matched perfectly!*

Having been born nearly 60 years ago and raised in Oklahoma during a time of peace and prosperity, I paid little mind to the goings on in the world during my first 12-15 years. I do remember people with bomb shelters in their back yard, but none as I recall in Oklahoma, I always felt the dangerous part of the World was a long ways off. Somehow it just didn't seem possible to us here in the heartland, that there are people in this world who want to kill us, just because of who we are and what we stand for. I am one of the Baby Boomers, a member of a generation born after

Rick Teal

World War II, but before the electronic age really began. I can remember our first TV set, Black and White, that received two channels. Wow were we uptown or what?

It was days of Little League, paper routes, and sock hops. One of the most vivid memories of my early childhood took place in (I believe 1957), when I was 9 years old. It was a lazy, hazy, summer and I remember well how we could see the Northern Lights (Aurora Borealis) all the way down here in Northeast Oklahoma. Quite a spectacle, and one that led me into an early thirst for scientific knowledge. I have always been one that had to know and understand why things happened. What and Where just weren't enough, I had to know why. Always questioning, sometimes to the extent that teachers, parents, and employers became impatient and irritated (my wife still does). Just because someone said it, or because it has always been that way, have never been valid reasons to believe or take action, as far as I am concerned. After all NE Oklahoma is just across the line from the show me state of Missouri.

I recall a science project in my early high school years, in which I genetically altered a population of fruit flies (by selective breeding), until they became effectively immune to DDT. The premise that I had set out to substantiate was the law of Survival of the Fittest. Over the course of

Yellow Dogs and Fruit Flies

much of my sophomore year I spent my biology lab classes working on this project. It was truly amazing to watch this rapidly reproducing insect attain higher and higher levels of resistance to this insecticide, simply by killing off those more susceptible individuals before they had a chance to breed. This in turn led to the individual flies with the highest resistance to DDT, being allowed to control the genetic make up of the next generation. As the next generation was born, the same procedure was followed, by exposing the entire colony to DDT and keeping track of the time required to kill off the majority of flies, only allowing those longest living survivors to reproduce.

I was very much impressed by the results of that years project. Looking back, I realize that it was my Biology Teacher that Year (Mr. Paul Cottom, God rest his Soul), that led me and allowed me to make these discoveries for myself. But at the time I recall for first time, the sense of power I felt at my control over generations of insects, and the way I was in total control not only of which individual lived and died, but of the genetic direction this species was taking (in a controlled environment). So it was, that in the course of 7 (as I recall, it might have been more) generations, that not only did a generation of fruit flies become nearly impervious to DDT, but I for the first time felt empowered, and not at the mercy of the world around me. This must be akin in many ways to the power that the Terrorists must feel over the world around them.

Rick Teal

Right up to the time a suicide bomber detonates his bomb, or flies a plane into the World Trade Center, he must be feeling an awesome since of empowerment.

In the society that many of these terrorists come from, a world with little hope of ever being in a position of power, this must be a real rush. I recall 1963 and that day in High School when John Kennedy was assassinated. It seemed surreal to so many of us that something like this could happen in our protected little world. I wasn't old enough to recall Pearl Harbor, but I remember the teachers at my school and my parents making reference to the shock over the Kennedy assassination in terms of the shock they felt over Pearl Harbor. This was probably the first time many of us had our secure little foundations shaken, but certainly not the last.

A few years later, as I graduated from High School, trying to decide what to do with the rest of eternity (I say eternity, because at that time I fully intended to live forever). I was of course interested in the draft, and Military service, as it was one of the topics foremost on the minds of young men in my generation. Viet Nam was on the 6 o'clock news every evening. So many of my generation felt that our government during the middle 60's didn't have our best interests at heart. I vividly remember Johnson's speech when he announced that he would not seek, nor would

Yellow Dogs and Fruit Flies

he accept the nomination of the democratic party for another term. It was a time when many of the youth asked why if he wasn't able to stay the course in our war, why should we?

Many of my peers chose to graduate and enlist or volunteer for the draft. I was one of the ones that decided to attend our community college, worked part time jobs, got married, and eventually joined the Oklahoma Army National Guard in order to continue my education, during which time our National involvement in Viet Nam came to an end. So for many of us during the late 60's and early 70's, dodging the draft was not a means to an end (as it was to some of those who fled to Canada or Europe with no intention of ever serving), it was a postponement to finish other requirements and priorities in our lives.

One of the truly great things about our country, is that individual choice can be applied even to issues of national significance, without having the moral police shooting at you. I would also take umbrage with those who mistakenly compare serving the in National Guard or Reserves with shirking a commitment to our countries military. As an old Oklahoma Army National Guard, Infantry 1st Sergeant, who spent over 20 years committed to this countries military, I can toll you that being on call and not being called can be very frustrating. To spend year after year training for the day you need that military expertise in a combat situation, then not being called, I would equate with always a bridesmaid, never a bride. Don't get me wrong, not many would say they look forward to deployment, but we all were ready to serve if called upon. As a matter of fact, many of the soldiers in Iraq and Afghanistan today are National Guard and Reservists. Many of the jobs required on a daily basis to support our troops there will be found primarily in reserve status. So many of the transportation units, medical units, and much of the close air support are provided by Reserve units called to active duty.

I don't think it is as common knowledge in this country as it should be, but the United States military has been operating on what we called the Total Force concept for many years now. That is a concept where the Reserves are considered an integral part of our overall defense structure. It is all about money. It costs much less to train and maintain a reserve army than an active component. When I hear media talking heads going on and on about re-instituting the Draft, I can only laugh at their ignorance and total lack of understanding of that of which they speak! It merely points out, that they have no personal knowledge of the military, (or more succinctly stated, they probably haven't served in the military). Since the end of the Viet Nam era, our military has undergone radical changes in structure (the Total Force Concept), Technological advancement of weapons systems (in Viet Nam the weapons we used were by no

Yellow Dogs and Fruit Flies

means smart), and changes from the World War II tactics that became obsolete with these technological changes. There is no need for storming the beaches into the face of machine gun fire, in today's modern warfare. I am not saying it isn't dangerous or just as deadly, I merely make the point that it is quite different. Even with years of training in reserve status, it requires months of intense training up, to attain readiness for active combat operations.

These high tech weapons systems, and the tactical sophistication of our troops has long since made the draft obsolete. Drafted soldiers lack the motivation, desire, and mission oriented training required to compete on today's battlefield. Less than 30% of the draftees of the 60's or 70's would qualify to enlist today. What are we going to do? Lower our standards to make way for drafting people into a military whose necessary standards require a higher quality. Make no mistake, as with those fruit flies, soldiers are competing on the battlefield to become the fittest to survive. The U.S. military no longer requires cannon fodder. Much of the rhetoric we here from the left today as they harp on re-instituting the draft, is their desire to involve rich young men as well as the middleclass in combat, we don't need class warfare in this country, just so Charlie Rengle can get re-elected. I would simply put it to those left wingers in Congress, that they should spend their time trying to make this country something that we all want to fight for, a place worthy of our young people's sacrifices, this is not an issue that my party should be trying to politicize. All we need is a few more Ted Kennedys or Hillary Clintons, and no one will find this country worth fighting for. Class warfare amongst Americans is not healthy nor justified.

It is up to you and I as taxpayer's (through our elected representation), to decide what level of readiness, and in what strength, we want to pay for. What strength levels on active duty will be required to fight this War on Terror? What strength levels can be maintained on reserve status until needed? The drawback to keeping a lower cost, higher percentage of our Total Force in reserve status, is the time required to *train up* to mission readiness status. We have to realize we get what we pay for. As with everything else in this world, if you want answers, just follow the money. The draft is not the answer, in fact it is not needed. Recruiting and Retention statistics are good, what we have to decide is what do we do away with in order to pay for a larger standing army, if that is what is needed. How can we ever come up with the right answers, if we don't ask the right questions.

Follow the Money is Rick's Lesson for this chapter. I will try to draw at least one irrefutable truth, something that life has taught me, out of each chapter, and that is the lesson for this one.

Yellow Dogs and Fruit Flies

No matter how convoluted the path to the truth may be, it can nearly always be tracked down by following the money trail. In a capitalist society, power is defined in dollars and cents.

$$$ FOLLOW THE MONEY $$$. Our capitalistic system is based on the value of commodities. For many years, we and the world, were on the gold standard, that is we based the value of our worth as a society, on the amount of gold (a commodity) that we could control (own). I remember one of the James Bond movies (GoldFinger as I recall) where the bad guys were going to increase their wealth, not by stealing our gold, but by making it inaccessible to us (a nuclear explosion and fallout inside Fort Knox was their plan). This was an attempt to offset the balance of power by a terrorist act. All fiction, and at the time quite entertaining.

Think about it though in today's terms. What if Terrorists today are able to make our new gold (we are now on the Oil Standard, and have been for many years), our insatiable thirst for energy and oil, unattainable, or so expensive that it changes the way we live. This would indeed have the same effect on us as stealing Fort Knox. We would have to make major revisions to our way of life. We could no longer own SUV's it would be back to the Yugo for most of us, we couldn't drive all over the countryside on the weekend just for the heck of it. Fewer trips to the store, carpooling to work, living closer to your job, wearing sweaters in the house all winter, living in 800 square feet instead of 8000 square feet, consuming less because the costs of production would increase dramatically. We would not see 18 Wheelers running up and down the interstates with next day delivery. We would again spend weeks and months waiting for delivery by rail or sea. It would mean drastic changes to our society that has become based on instant gratification of all wants, needs, and desires.

It might not be all bad though, as it might at the very least help us restrain our children from their head long rush to bankruptcy. I personally feel that the availability of easy credit to kids still in high school and college, is sinful. It allows the now generation to become so indebted by the time they are 25 years old that they may never see the end of the debt tunnel. It is another devious plot to enslave this countries youth. Too many kids today are totally disinterested in what a car or a house costs, their only concern is how much is the payment. Satan is truly at work in our society as he enslaves our youth to their own greediness and insatiable thirst for things.

But to return to my story, in the late 60's and early 70's, I finished High School, Graduated from College, got married, raised a family worked two jobs, and retired from the National Guard just after the end of the first Gulf War. I wasn't called

Yellow Dogs and Fruit Flies

into that war as it ended too quickly for any but a few National Guard or Reservists to be called (Too bad, it would have been much easier, less expensive, and would have saved lives had we in retrospect gone to Baghdad in '91). At that time however, we were more interested in appeasing the Saudi royal family to keep the oil flowing, than we were in deposing Sadam, and fighting Terrorism which was just a blip on the radar screen then. In the next chapter I am going to talk about Terrorism extensively, and my take on the why's and wherefores, but before we begin that discussion, I think it is imperative that we discuss the Saudis.

Saudi Arabia has been a force to contend with for less than 50 years. Up until shortly after World War II, and the demand for more and more energy, Saudi Arabia was a backward place straight out of *Ali Baba And The Forty Thieves. Laurence of Arabia* was the setting that most of the west took for granted as the Arab world. A bunch of Nomads riding camels and killing each other over the rights to camp next to the sweetest water hole. The Saudi Royal family has for centuries embraced the most restrictive form of Islamic teachings. It has done this in order to continue it's total control and domination of the population of Saudi Arabia and also it's oil. Today the schools in Saudi Arabia spend much more time teaching the fundamentalist Islamic teachings than they do math or science, even to the extent of publicly flogging teachers who teach anything deemed by the Religious clerics to be adverse to the laws of Islam (regardless of the scientific truthfulness of it). What couldn't happen in an open society that recognizes freedom of the individual to think and speak, independently of government, is rife in Saudi Arabia.

By looking at the Scopes Monkey trial of the 30's right here in the good old U.S. of A. you can see how free thought will generally always prevail over religious zealotry in this country.

Add this to the ability the Internet has given us, that of any individual, to go *on line* and find plans to bombs, information on terror cells, and ability to raise funds, and you have a recipe for Terror the likes of which the world has never seen before. It has only been since the Oil standard became the measure of wealth of the Western world, that the huge reserves under the Saudi dessert have given rise to so much power for the Saudi Royal family. The easy to say, but much more difficult to do answer, is simply get off the oil standard, and the power of the Saudi's and their ability to control so much of our daily world will go away nearly immediately. At nearly 60 years of age, one of my greatest regrets, is that I did not become a world class energy scientist and discover the next centuries answer to the energy crisis.

Chapter #2
More on Terrorism

Reader's Cramp Relief: *Did you hear about the terrorist who went deer hunting in the mountains of Afghanistan? After he shot a large buck, he grabbed an antler and began dragging it through the underbrush. He struggled mightily, continually having to stop and untangle the antlers from the underbrush. Finally he ran into Usama Bin Laden, who offered to help, and advised that if they would drag the dead deer by its rear hooves, instead of the antler's it would be less likely to become so entangled in the brush. So with his help the terrorist moved out making good time dragging the deer by his heels. After several hours though Bin Laden stopped to rest and noted how much easier it wais dragging the deer by its heels. The Terrorist agreed that it is easier but we sure are getting a long ways from my truck!*

Ideally we should STOP Terrorism before it happens (by what ever means)

If we can't do that, we should Take Justice to the Terrorists

Rick Teal

Only then as a last resort, should we bring the Terrorists to Justice.

I fail to understand how US citizens can become so faint of heart and feel such resolute sympathy for people who want to kill us. Those combatants now detained in Guantanamo, were captured on the battlefields of the War on Terror. As such they are detainees, and prisoners of war, not detainees of our US judicial system, and in no way entitled to the rights of an American judicial prisoner. To try and lump them into the same category is ridiculous. The reason, the only reason that we take prisoners of war, is the same reason that we kill enemy combatants on the battlefield, to keep them from killing us! Here again the Bleeding Heart Liberals that want to take them back to Afghanistan and try them for their crimes are wrong headed. We might as well issue them weapons and give them a ride to our front lines so they can run out in no man's land and turn around and start shooting at us again.

Fighting Terror everywhere in the World is the Fourth World War. We cannot afford nor allow terrorism to strike and then take action. If we don't fight Global Terror where it lives, we will be fighting it here. If we learned nothing else September 11 2001, we should have learned that one undeniable truth. There is evil in the world, and it wants to kill us. You and I are on the hit list, and only taking the fight to them will keep them from continuing

Yellow Dogs and Fruit Flies

to bring it to us. This is a struggle more important than any that we have faced, since the end of the Third World War, which was the Cold War with the Soviets.

During our 40 years War (50's, 60's, 70's, and 80's) or the Cold War as it was called, the United States struggled against the Evil Empire. We had a real Walking Talking Enemy, *"The Russians are Coming"*. We could see them, We had weapons poised and pointed at each other, sometimes (as with the Cuban Missile Crises), they were close enough to smell. For nearly 40 years, there were few shots fired (at least not openly) between the major combatants, although many surrogate targets were used. This policy of waging a non-shooting war was called Detante'.

Detante' (not surprisingly, this is a French word), didn't work in the 60's and 70's, and it won't work now. Detante' the alternative to real combat during the cold war, was to weaken ourselves militarily, so that we all remained at the same level of armament, (a Mexican standoff so to speak). For years our policy was that if we all had the same number of bullets in our guns, we would both be afraid to shoot, because if we missed we'd be outgunned, or some such nonsense. This alternative to killing each other was dreamed up in order to bury our heads and not face up to Nuclear Holocaust and what it would mean. But it is imperative to face up to the fact that it was not really a deterrent to anything. It only meant that each side had to keep escalating in order to stay ahead of our foe. Putting a man on the Moon was one of the few positive things to come out of the Space Race, which was just another battle in the Cold War.

We only defeated the Soviets (World War III) by outspending them, by producing in the 80's the most powerful economy and military machine that the world had ever seen. We forced the Soviets and their Military machine to become economically unable to continue competing with us on a global scale. We out bought them, we out produced them, and we broke their will to continue. The Berlin Wall came down and the rest is history! It is Ironic, that the very country, Germany, that our war machine protected for all those years, is one of our major detractors now due to their behind the scenes nefarious dealings with Iraq and the oil for food scam.

If we in this country, feel our military machine is over deployed now, it is because we have not re-evaluated so many of the places that troops are deployed in, that may no longer be necessary. Germany and Western Europe are probably among them. Why do we continue to maintain a cold war level of bases and troops, in Germany? Let the French and Germans begin paying for their own national defense and see how quickly their attitudes towards us change. Allies come and

Yellow Dogs and Fruit Flies

allies go, continuing to court the likes of France and Germany, is redundant. As with the United Nations and the food for oil scheme, they have made themselves irrelevant by their dealings with Sadam and Iraq.

The Cold War was not won because we gave in and appeased the Soviets; it was won because we brought them to their knees economically, so that their own citizens demanded change. So that their own citizens saw the disparity between their society and ours, ours that was based on taxpayers paying less to support it than theirs, but yet a higher standard of living, ours that was brought on by individuals having the freedom to express themselves, but the responsibility of providing for themselves. Freedom indeed isn't free, it costs lives and dollars and national will to preserver. I am proud to be an American, and yes I'm proud to be a Cowboy! I become furious when European leaders look down their noses at us because we continually prove to them just how weak their position has become. I really liked what our Secretary of State said in the run up to the Iraq war, when he made reference to the Old Europe. What he was saying was it really was irrelevant what France and Germany thought of our intentions, they had after all been in the pocket of Sadam for years and had become insignificant as allies anyway.

Rick Teal

After we have spent so many lives and dollars dragging their sorry, cowardly butts out of one fire after another they try to submarine us at the UN. I guess it can best be explained by a simple analogy. Have you loaned money to a friend? Have they paid it back? If the answer is NO, they probably are no longer a friend. They resent you because they feel guilty whenever you are around, and you resent them for being weak and unable to get out of their own messes. You feel you have a financial right to tell them how to live after all they owe you money. And they feel you are a nosey SOB that should mind your own business, and you can take your IOU and stick it where the sun don't shine. Neither a Lender nor Borrower be. Advice for all ages.

And that is Rick's lesson for this chapter: We can't buy friendship. After literally decades of using our power, money, and national will, to help poor downtrodden societies around the world become better places for their man on the street to live, we should see the handwriting on the wall. We need only look at human nature to see that giving things to people does not make them like you. On the contrary it makes them feel bad that they are now beholden to you, so they either want to stay out of your company, or more than likely, they will try for the rest of their lives to prove that you are no better than them, by trying to bring you down to their level. This is one reason I am so afraid of John Kerry's campaign for the

Yellow Dogs and Fruit Flies

presidency, I think he really and truly believes that impressing the European community is more important than protecting ours.

I can still remember what it was like as a young man, not to be as popular as so many of my classmates in Junior High School. I don't mean to say I was the last one picked in all the games but I rightly or wrongly perceived myself as less popular. While I wasn't ostracized, neither was I accepted into the inner circle, that was reserved for our Football sports heros. I was resentful of them, and very skeptical and suspicious when later in high school I became popular as the guy that had a fast car. For that reason, I often did not give the popular kids a fair shake. Not because of anything they had personally done to me, but because of my own perceived ideas of them. I think this is something that we can all in one way or another sympathize with. Whether we were personally not popular because of our zits, or ostracized because we were poor and couldn't wear the *in* styles, we have all felt at one time or another that we were on the outside looking in. That we weren't accepted or appreciated by our peers. As I look back now I realize that most of those people I sometimes felt inferior to then were not such a much. In fact some of the people I went to school with may have had a full six pack, but they were missing the plastic thingy that holds them together. This same uneasiness takes

Rick Teal

place between nations and quite often can lead to conflict or even wars.

Which brings up another sore spot, the United Nations is not designed to act in the best interests of the United States. The UN is still trying to operate as it has since 1945. It is no longer valid, and I for one do not believe in one world government. One only need recount some of the horror stories of the whims and vagaries of our Federal bureaucracy to realize how terrible it would be to centralize that kind of power over the world in one place. John Kerry has made it clear since the early 70's, that he was a proponent of one world government. That he really believed that we should never take unilateral action, even if it is in our best interests. That we should submit to United Nations rules, regulations, never taking action unless the rest of the World says it is ok. Does he really think that we should listen to nations that we have to support with our foreign aid before we act? I sometimes think the man has two brains, one is lost and he's looking for the other (just can't decide which one to think with today). It's hard to believe he beat out 1 million other sperm, little lone the seven dwarves for my parties nomination for president.

The world never has and never will be ruled by committee. It will be ruled by the strongest. As with the fruit fly, Survival of the Fittest, is one of God's unalterable truths. The Big eat the little, the Strong control the weak, and the Meek will inherit

Yellow Dogs and Fruit Flies

the earth in Heaven, and not one millisecond before. So Good can only overcome Evil with a liberal dose of perseverance, national will, and gunpowder. Put another way, in the words of a song from World War II "Praise the Lord and Pass the Ammunition". Or as Teddy Roosevelt said "Walk Softly but Carry a Big Stick". It is being called the Bush Doctrine, and will probably be the defining statement of his Presidency. Basically, it says don't wait until we are injured to take action. Use what ever resources are needed, to see to it that we make every effort to keep terrorists from hurting us. Creation of the Department of Homeland Security, and taking preemptive actions in Afghanistan, Iraq, and anyplace else it is needed, is in our best interests.

The Bush Doctrine

Premise #1: Pre-empt Terrorism whenever and wherever possible by the use of unilateral force if necessary!!!

Premise #2: You are either with us or against us,

Terror can only be waged against us, if we allow it to take root in our hearts and minds. Truly FREE men cannot be terrorized. If we all strive to be courageous, the terror cannot harm us. It might kill us, but it can't harm us. What I am trying

Rick Teal

to say is that a truly free person is not afraid of the unknown. The old Viking analogy that Only the Rocks Live Forever, may say it best. We are all in this World for a finite time. It is not the length of that time that defines the quality of our lives, but rather what we accomplish with the time we are allotted. Those of us who are afraid of dying are for the most part afraid of living, afraid of the unknown. That's where the strength of one's faith comes into play. It is difficult to look into the depths of the unknown, if you don't have some faith in what will be found on the other side whether the unknown you are looking at is a river, a war, or your own mortality.

Terror is a state of mind, I choose not to live that way. I will not allow fear to rule me, therefore I cannot be terrorized. We have seen this attitude clearly, in the manner in which the citizens of Israel have handled their situation. It is a testament to their beliefs, that they do not allow acts of terrorism to deter how they live their everyday lives. Peace in the Middle East can only be approached, when both sides in the issue come to realize that terror can never prevail. Only when the world quits making Religion the basis for how we govern ourselves, can we ever be free of terrorists, but on the other hand, we have to understand how important faith is to the individuals state of mind.

It is amazing to me how the value of the lives of Arabs has so drastically increased since Sadam is

Yellow Dogs and Fruit Flies

no longer the abuser. I do not condone the acts of the US Military in committing acts of abuse on Iraqi prisoners (whether they deserve it or not, it is not for guards to decide). But I am truly astonished at the level of vitriol being leveled by the world press, when they were so callously willing to overlook much worse abuses by the government of Iraq under Sadam! From Rape rooms, to gassing the Kurds, to cutting out tongues and on and on, where was this Worldwide outrage then?? Where was the media while this was taking place?? And by the way, if it means saving one American life, I have no problem with using hooding, intimidation, humiliation, or other effective interrogation techniques to extract information from criminals and terrorists.

Our world is divided into religious sectors and areas, where different cultures view our time on earth and afterwards, differently. Generally Northern Africa, the Middle East and much of SW Asia are Muslim Countries, While the West for the Most Part is Christian and Jewish. The latter Religions while not being the same are at least compatible and based on the same doctrines established in the Old Testament of the Bible. The Islamic Religion on the other hand is based on the Koran, a different version of many of the same Biblical stories and lessons, but written from the perspective of a different civilization. A civilization based on a Nomadic life style where no real since of Nationalism exists. A civilization that for countless centuries has changed very little. A civilization that until the last half of the 20th century had not even formed governments as they are known today. In Afghanistan today, as in many of the Arab countries, tribal leaders very loosely associated at the national level by religion only, make up the governing bodies of those nations. These are the nations that make up much of the United Nations, these are the nations (with little or no national identity as we tend to think of it), that we are depending on to help us run the world.

Religion is an example of a very personal thing becoming the basis of a National or International view of the world. While all individuals will have a slightly different belief within the wide view of a given religion (often based on individual life experiences) They will also of necessity be expected to adhere to basic truths of that given religion. Whether these basic practices are good or bad, depends on your perspective, but they are necessary to the overall acceptance of a Religion and its long term well being.

Organized Religion is certainly one of the most serious dangers in the World today. I think we in the West are missing a very important distinction, not because our religion is better or worse, but because of one of our most important principals, the separation of Church and State. Now I am not going to become a card carrying member of the ACLU over this, and I fully believe that our

Yellow Dogs and Fruit Flies

government was formed as One Nation Under God, and I will fight and die if need be to keep it that way. But the real underlying reason for the emphasis by our Founding Fathers in keeping a distinct distance between government and religion was to set a barrier in place that would not allow religious control of government not the other way around. Our founding fathers were all Christians, and sought to make God an integral part of our Christian country.

It was done to give every religion the same right to be heard without giving any religion control over me and you. Notice I didn't say all religions should have equal time, or equal emphasis, that will be up to the given religion to sell itself). For instance, I don't think that a religion that believes in snake worship should be able to force me to kiss a snake, on the other hand if that trips your trigger, kiss away. Some people can be led anywhere, the rest of us can't become too upset by their fates. Face it, the world is full of **Kool Aid** drinkers, people that can not distinguish between what's real and what is make believe. Kids that play electronic games to the exclusion of being able to function in the real world fall into that category. Shame on their parents for making that illusion an alternative for them. I mean there are idiots all over, we don't have to sanction their lives, or feel that they have equal rights. I know a lady who once got on to me for unscrewing a light bulb rather than turning off the switch, she said I was wasting electricity. These folks do have a right to an equal opportunity, but what they do with it is up to them.

But back to religious beliefs being forced on others. In other parts of the world however this distinction is not only not present, it is actively opposed by Religious leadership. They are currently in control of governments in most of the Arab world, and will give it up only over their cold, dead bodies. They will use any means available to them including Terrorism to prevent any movement toward self government or individualism or a democratic society. Religious Oligarchies in the Arab World recognize that having a freely formed democratic state in their midst will in time be the death Nell of their civilizations as they are currently known.

Religious Zealots in power around the world, are using the religious beliefs of their populations, and total control over education, to recruit and train ordinary Muslims to become the Crazies and Fanatics who are willing to die in order to confront us. It is an easy sell they only have to teach them to hate. The other part of the puzzle that until the past 50 years has not been a viable concern, is Weapons of Mass Destruction (WMD). WMD make it possible for one fanatic to kill 1000's of innocents in the name of religion or any other silly ass reason they can think of. This is a new concept to the World, it only takes one nut with a

Yellow Dogs and Fruit Flies

bottle of anthrax, or an atomic bomb in a suitcase, to literally ignite the world. People the world over favor underdogs, but they follow the top dogs. The biggest ideas of the biggest men in the world, can be shot down by the smallest men with the smallest minds. What we spend years building can be torn down in a millisecond.

Why do they hate us? Why are seemingly ordinary believers of Islam willing to die to kill us? Think about it, When believers of Islam look at the West (Jews and Christians), and see our standard of living, and our open and free societies, and ask their religious leaders why there is such a disparity? Why can't I have a new car, and a three bedroom house? Where is my share of the pie? I pray daily, I perform all the rituals you have told me to, I live a good Muslim life. Why do those heathen Americans get all the breaks? When you look at it, their upper middle class lives in squalor, compared to the low income poor in the west. The only answer they can believe, the only one that will allow that religious oligarchy to maintain it's strangle hole on its population: We in the West are the Devil. We are the infidels; there can be no other answer that allows them to continue selling their brand of religion to the masses, that allows poor misguided Muslims to retain their religious beliefs.

Any other point of view would be to break faith with their religion, which so often is the only thing

Rick Teal

they have left. It must be an undeniable truth to them, that we are the evil empire, or they could no longer retain their religion or beliefs, and would become lost in chaos. So they are taught from an early age to hate us, they are taught that they should not aspire to the same goals that we do, not because they are unatainable, but because they are unatainable within the restraints of their Islamic beliefs.

Now also consider that they live not in a free open society, where choices are freely presented, but in a religious state. A place where there is no freedom of religion, you either believe the way the Religion driven State tells you to, or you probably won't live long. A State where religion is taught in schools with a higher priority than math or science. A Religious State that teaches its children and actively promotes becoming a Martyr.

I think most of us in the west understand that this culture needs help moving into the 21st century, but remember many times the people you help will attack you when you do. They will resent you for the fact that they require your assistance, but we have to help them anyway if not for them then for our own good. The world has grown too small to think that distance or oceans can protect us from small minds with big grudges and Weapons of Mass Destruction.

Yellow Dogs and Fruit Flies

In these States whose Religious leaders actively promote dying in order to kill the infidel (us) look at what they are promised. Martyrdom brings 72 virgins and wealth untold in the next life, a better place where a martyr will no longer have to worry about the standard of living of himself or his family. Dying for your religion is an honor, a duty, and oh by the way, Mr. Sadam Hussien is going to make your family rich also. So you have a great afterlife which you can begin now, and your family can also start living better right here on good old Planet Earth.

So we see young people, they often times don't even know what a virgin is, but it must be good, they have no real concept of dying, (that's why young men make the best soldiers), and with no real hope for the future anyway what do they have to lose? So they strap dynamite to their chests, get on a crowded bus, and blow themselves up. Not so difficult to understand their motivation when you look at their alternatives. And all this is supported, paid for, and even promoted by Religious Governments.

The only hope we in our Western culture have is to overcome centuries of hate and religious teachings that clearly promote and encourage the average Muslim to die in order to kill us. The only way this can take place is to get rid of the leadership of these Religious dictatorships. To either kill them, or expose them for what they are, and assist (as we have in Iraq), their populations to rebel. The assassinations of radical Hamas leaders in Israel is a course of action that should be applauded in the Western world, not condemned. The most rapid way of breaking the stranglehold of radical religious leaders on their populations is to quit killing soldiers, and begin killing their leaders. Making it clear that any leader who promotes such actions will become a target in our war on terror. If we kill enough leaders, there will be no soldiers left to kill. Killing leaders will actually save lives in the long run as well as enabling the populations to begin self rule based on democratic ideals. Sometimes you give your best and get kicked in the teeth for your trouble, but we still have to give our best anyway. It's the American way to give our best at all times.

Hamas is only one of the terrorist organizations that we have to get rid of, but in all cases, they have to be handled the same way as you handle a snake. Cut off the head and the rest of the snake dies. These are governments and regions that are held in the iron grip of the past, supported by Terrorists and other bullies who will kill their own citizens with impunity in order to solidify their power. Countries with no chance of modernization unless we become involved and provide assistance in the way of military support. This is not an option, this is not something that we can choose to do or not, if we do not act now, this cancer in the World can only spread, and eventually scar and deface the

Yellow Dogs and Fruit Flies

entire planet. We are truly in the middle of World War IV.

If indeed it is our destiny to rule the world as the only super power, then let us do so in a way that spreads democracy, and self rule. Let us truly, once and for all make the World safe for democracy. That was our stated goal not so many years ago. How have we so drastically lost that objective?

We the People, of the United States of America, are in the drivers seat, as the last super power. We must wield that power wisely, and that includes refusing to abdicate our responsibility to the citizens of the World. We have to take on the role of the guiding light for the rest of civilization to shine by. Not a role I relish, but one we cannot shirk from. Do you think for one minute that God has bestowed the highest standard of living in the world and all of the blessings He has so we can waste it? I think not, I think God is making it very clear that there is a real War going on, and we have been put in the unenviable position of upholding and enforcing His Will.

It is time for us to choose. This will be the single most important election that most of us will ever participate in. We must decide whether to attack Terrorism where it lives (in the Middle East, one need only look at a world map to see the threat) or to again try to appease people who

Rick Teal

clearly can't be appeased. The governments in the Muslim countries of the world are for the most part despotic dictatorships, or feudal kingdoms, where the opinions of a few control the lives of millions.

How can we be so naïve as to think that the lip service being paid by those despots to democracy is real. It is clear to me that the United Nations is an organization controlled by those same despots or their contractors {France, Germany, Russia all involved in the food for oil scam}. Those Arab countries whose despotic governments often openly fund the terrorist movement.

That is the importance of the portion of the Bush Doctrine, that states you are either with us or against us. The only option that dictators and kings have in order to maintain their positions of power, is to defeat us.

It is not too difficult to realize as most of these terrorist governments must, that to attack us openly nation vs. nation, would be suicide. The only option they are left with then is subsidizing terrorists to break our will. To make us afraid to continue to confront them.

To paraphrase Winston Churchill, The only thing we have to fear is fear itself. Refuse to give in to fear, vote this year for the kind of government

Yellow Dogs and Fruit Flies

that refuses to be intimidated by thugs, thieves, and terrorists.

Chapter 3
The MEDIA

Reader's Cramp Relief: *A reporter flying to Europe to cover a story was stopped by Airport Security for a baggage check. After it was x-rayed, the security guard ask if anyone put anything into his baggage without his knowledge? To which the reporter replied impatiently, If it was without my knowledge how would I know? The security guard shook her head knowingly and replied "That's why we ask!".*

It is high time we quit trying to hire the government to make us be good to each other. All it get's us is higher taxes, more laws, and lower quality of citizens. If I make a million dollars, it belongs to me, not some bureaucrat wanting to give it to people that refuse to take personal responsibility for themselves. Remember the Fruit Fly! I have the right not to be tolerant of dead beats and their offspring. If we continue providing for those deadbeats based on the number of progeny they produce, we will continue watering down the genetics of our culture until there is no one left fit to survive. There are already too many people in

Yellow Dogs and Fruit Flies

the gene pool that slipped in when the life guard wasn't looking.

We are a divided country due in large part because we have a divided media. While the sound of reason, and the voice of the silent majority is no longer silent the voice of the Mass media has become distorted by greed and a lust for power, and can no longer be trusted to give unbiased accounts of the news for us to interpret. We are subjected to sound bite news stories where those parts of the news that do not support the Newscasters point of view are quite often withheld. What is unsaid is as important as what is said, and the listener has to constantly be on guard to try and pick out the real information. We can no longer trust that what is being touted on the 6 O'clock news is accurate, nor can we conclude that no one is using their news broadcast to advance an agenda. Why has this become so important?? Why is the will of the people no longer the most important priority to our mass media?

Rick's Lesson for Chapter 3: Taxation without Representation. The people who vote are not the people who necessarily pay for the government. Many of our Congressional leaders are bandying about the idea of re-instating the draft for military service. Well let's face it, we already have a draft. Every year on the 1st of January, working Americans are drafted for 5 months national service. They are drafted to provide for those people who choose not to provide for themselves. Let's not forget the fruit flies, and the lessons of survival of the fittest. If a person chooses not to work, then they also choose not to eat, therefore they choose not to live, which rapidly solves the problem of people not willing to work being a burden on the rest of us. Also remember that people to whom we give things, will resent us for the gift.

How can we expect those who pay to support our government, to be willing to let someone else control it. How do seemingly intelligent hardworking Americans allow those who don't work and don't pay taxes to run our country? By listening to the media owned by and controlled by special interests. Americans who trust the national news media for a fair unbiased view of the world, are being led down the garden path because and it is not in the best interests of special interests, for you to always have accurate accounts of the news. Voters are not necessarily taxpayers, and that is a monumental problem, in a democratic society, where the majority rules. What happens when 51% of voters are no longer required to pay taxes? Why do you suppose that our national Democratic party has sold its soul to the poor, minority, illegal immigrants, environmentalists, and other special interests, who vote without being required to pay for the activities they vote for? Who says that our government is paid for by the people who support it? Should those who don't own land be allowed to vote to raise property taxes? Should those who don't work be allowed to raise income taxes? I'll take this up in more detail later.

But for the time being let us consider for example: If the Percentage of taxpayers interested in AIDS research are outnumbered by those who are interested in Alzhiemers research, then it would stand to reason that Alzhiemers research would receive the major portion of government funding available for research. Majority rules right? This is a basic principle of a republic, that such decisions be left to the majority to rule. Enter the mass media, and in this example consider that it is in the best interests of the Mass media to see that AIDS receives the research moneys, then they could (and conceivably do) use their considerable influence with the 6 o'clock news to convince your government to fund AIDS research, even though the majority would be better off with Alzhiemers research.

How do they do this? Can they directly control how your government works?

No, they have to have your assistance in this duplicity. You have to be actively involved in your own worst interests. You have to actively tell your legislators to Fund AIDS research, or you will no longer support them. And since getting re-elected is the goal of nearly all of our national politicians, they will listen to those of you who can convince them that you represent enough voters to cast them out if they don't go along with your wishes. Let's face it, if you are given the choice of deciding what services you will be given, with no requirement to help pay for it, what would you do?

So when you watch the news, and hear that bad people are supporting Alzhiemers research and good people are supporting AIDS research, read between the lines (or I should say listen to what is really being said). Ask yourself, what really is your priority, ask yourself who these bad people really are, and are they really bad by your definition, or just that of your news commentator, who may have AIDS and not Alzhiemers. Although I have to think that only some form of dementia can explain Andy Rooney's ridiculous comments of late! Andy you donated your brain to science to soon.

We also need to grasp the perspective of most (if not all) of the national media's take on who they want to see in power in this country, and why. For the most part, very few people are a part of the World power base. In other words, very few real people have real input into how the world operates. You either have to be one of the ones whose money makes you powerful, (Bill Gates probably is close to one, The Arab royal family is certainly one (notice they have the status of only one, and have to act that way), or a person who

Yellow Dogs and Fruit Flies

has the innate ability to influence those with money (Usama Bin Laden is what I would characterize as a charismatic leader), or a person who can sway the opinions/beliefs of a Nation or Region of the World (US Presidents (or their administrations), and some Islamic Clerics, are examples of this group). Everyone else is on the outside looking in, including the Media Moguls (with the possible exceptions of Ted Turner, CNN, who has the money to make him a marginal power brokers, at least in the US).

Now consider if you will, how a National News Commentator like a Dan Rather or a Walter Cronkite or any of a dozen of the other Liberal thinkers must feel. Always so near the top of the elite field, able to hob knob with the powerful, but without the real power or money (even though they may be quite well off, they are not in that class) to have real sway over those few who rule the world. It has been said that there are only 1000 people in the world, meaning that at any given time, the way of the world is controlled by 1000 people of means and power. These Media elite are close to power all the time, they need to feel that they can exercise some control over the things they deal with, that those in power actually hear and respect what they have to say, simply by virtue of the National Media which they can mold to their own ideas. I am not saying they are power mongers, I am saying that they deal at the fringe of power, with no real prospect of ever wielding

Rick Teal

any. (look out, I hear Tom Brokaw would like to be Vice President).

Now along comes the cowboy from Texas, who really doesn't have much use for the national media. He pays them very little mind, and not much more lip service. He doesn't go out of his way (he or his administration), to make Tom, and Dan or anyone in the White House press corps feel needed. They don't feel like they are getting the proper respect. They're being snubbed, and shown to be not very important after all in the real world (which they aren't), and they don't like how it tastes or how it feels. So they take the approach of paybacks are hell, and try to use what limited power they have to sway the minds of the masses, in order to punish this administration for not being properly respectful of who they are! They've been shown up by this president, as not being nearly as important as they need everyone to think they are. They have truly forgotten what their job is. They no longer understand that their lot in life, the road that they have chosen to travel, demands that they act in a totally unbiased and fair manner in reporting facts, not innuendo. Just the facts mam. Opinions should be left to those who are asked, those in a position to know, and those whose opinions count. Those in the Media should remember their place, or be prepared to lose their market share (which is what seems to be taking place).

A president who doesn't treat his White house press corps with the respect they feel they should have. The president in a press conference to defend his actions in going to Iraq, was not questioned on the substantive issues of the day, but was lambasted repeatedly for refusing to accept responsibility for doing something wrong in the handling of Iraq (which according to subsequent polls, the American Public doesn't feel is necessary). The press on numerous occasions tried to force him to apologize to them for transgressions, which they and they alone perceived. I believe it had more to do with the fact that this president and this administration has had little use for the press, and has shown disdain for it (which also is a viewpoint shared by the majority of Americans).

Yes all of a sudden the major networks ABC, CBS, NBC, and even CNN, are losing their audience. Their percentage in the Nielsen is dropping (and has been for years) because the folks are tired of the same old rhetoric. Tired of Talking Heads with Agenda's. What ever happened to unbiased reporting? I for one do not require the assistance of Chris Mathews to understand what has been said in a speech. I am sick to death of the Liberal media trying to spin good news as bad and vice versa. Let's get back to calling a spade a spade, or else everyone will watch Fox news for unbiased reporting. Truth be known the majority already has switched off CNN, NBC, ABC, CBS etc. in favor of FOX news and listening to talk radio for their news and opinions.

Which brings up another interesting phenomenon, Liberal Talk radio is having to pay for its airtime, and sue in the courts to force radio stations to carry its message. Why? Because it can't pay its own way. Talk radio as with most other forms of media, has to be paid for by advertisers, people and companies that want to sell their goods and services to the listening public. Capitalism at its finest. So why is it that these so called Liberal Talk shows have to buy their air time? Because they don't command enough of a listener base (audience) to pay their own way and induce advertisers to buy their airtime for them, as they do for the conservative talk show format. Ought to tell someone something.

When did my party become the party of misery? How is it that only an increase in the depth of despair is a positive thing for my party? Why must even positive news by spun as bad by the democrats? John Kerry has even had to define his own misery index, because things aren't bad enough for him. Let's look at some real facts:

Real Job Growth for the last 3 nearly 4 quarters is the best in 30 years. How the National Media in cahoots with the Liberal National Democratic Agenda, can try to spin that as bad is a completely irrational process to me. It only proves what they

Yellow Dogs and Fruit Flies

truly think, that the average American is dumb as a rock, and will timidly be led (hopefully to the polls), with no ability to think for ourselves.

It is one of the things that makes me so angry with my party, and so many of the members of it, that it will allow people like Terry McAuliffe to lead it. That it will give national prominence to the ideas of the likes of Shawn Penn, George Clooney, Susan Sarandin, and other Hollywood types, that have never had to live in the real world in their lives. How the hell would they know. And who could possibly care what they think.

If you are one of those that does listen and believe what they say because they are famous, shame on you, you're a person that deserves what you get!

We have made great strides in Iraq, with more infrastucture in place now than before the War began, new schools, better power, water supplies, and even a new constitution. I hope everyone realizes what is at stake here. A strongly formed Democratic state in the middle of this hotbed known as the Middle East, will be the beginning of Peace in the Middle East.

Never has the opportunity been more available, or the road to peace more distinctly marked. I don't feel mission creep is taking place. A free middle

Rick Teal

east is the only way we will ever have peace not only in the region, but in the world. A free, self governed Middle East is the only recipe for real peace in our time.

I would even predict that as Afghanistan is stabilized, as Iraq is stabilized, that the other countries like Jordan, and Saudi Arabia are going to see the hand writing on the wall and fall into line by giving their citizens more and more control over their own lives. It is not just a coincidence, that Libya and Khadafi have seen the error of their ways, that they now are giving up their Weapons of Mass Destruction and making peace with their terrorist past. That Iran is beginning to allow Nuclear Inspections, that North Korea has decided that perhaps they should woo a peaceful solution with their neighbors or face the our wrath.

Never in the history of mankind, has a country so powerful as the United States existed. A power that can have such a far reaching effect, that could use that power to totally control the entire world if it so chooses, but has chosen to use it to do so much GOOD. I truly am Proud to be an American, and I consider myself a patriot. But I can also see why those enemies of freedom, those who truly despise and oppose the self-government by the masses, can so fear us as to find no other course but to try and destroy us. We are all citizens of the world, and as such we find ourselves at one of those rare historical cross roads, where the path

Yellow Dogs and Fruit Flies

we take over the next few years will control our destiny for the next few centuries. Do we move forward to a democratic world where the people have a say in their own lives? Or do we step back into anarchy, where war lords and local thugs can control the lives of those around them?

And while I am on the subject of Patriotism and being an American, I want to state what I see as a major difference in this centuries immigrant and last. This is a point where I disagree whole heartedly with George Bush. I did not spend 20 years in the Oklahoma National Guard, nor did my father and grand father fight in foreign conflicts, so illegal immigrants can leave their sorry countries to come here and abuse and disrespect ours. If you want to immigrate legally to this country, then do so knowing you will have to be assimilated into our culture, and that means learn the language. It is English. If you want to continue speaking a foreign tongue, do it in a foreign place.

Indeed, our constitution was not written so that you (or the liberal courts so dead set on protecting those from other lands), could come here and interpret it for us. Go interpret your own! You say you don't have one? Well Da! That's why you wanted to come huh? If you can't understand the word Stop in English, the police still have the right to shoot your sorry butt for not doing It. Ignorance of the law is no excuse. I am under no obligation to afford your non-English speaking children a non-English education, it's your place to see to it they can take advantage of what's in front of them. Yes you and they have an equal right to avail yourselves of the services our government provides. But we are in no way obligated to make special provisions so you can.

Chapter 4
The Economy

Reader's Cramp Relief: *At a Good bye luncheon for an old and dear co-worker, who was leaving the company due to "<u>Down Sizing</u>", a manager commented cheerfully, "This is fun. We should have these get-togethers more often."*

When you look at the real numbers, the Economy is better today than it was when Bush took office. This Recession we have been in began during the end of the nineties. It began for several reasons not the least of which was Unbridled greed on the part of Corporate America and was sustained for 5 years of the late 90's by unbridled greed on the part of investors. Sort of an AmWay pyramid type affair. The dot.coms were more than happy to make tons of money off of the greed of people who invested in electrons they could not see. I became alarmed early, when I recognized one day the dilemma taking place. My father and several of his coffee cronies, none of whom had anyb experience at all with computers, were talking about investing in the dot com revolution. Here were some old fella's who had worked hard and struggled all their lives willing to invest in something that they knew little or nothing about, just because other people were making a lot of money at it.

Investments in companies that basically had no real net worth (as in equipment and hard assets), was rampant. Anyone who could put up a web site and publish a balance sheet, could command respect on the stock market, for long enough for the CEO to sail away on a golden parachute. Reminds of the "***Emporer's new clothes***", no visible means of support was required by the often greedy investors of the early and mid 90's who expected double digit annual returns (and got them).

There was nothing of substance there, but everyone was afraid to say so. Then when someone did ask where the beef was, the entire house of cards came tumbling down, and all of those so called executives yanked the ripcord on their Golden Parachutes and retired to who knows where. Those who lost money at the end of the 90's, created much of their own problem by expecting unrealistic returns on investments, that could never be sustained over the long run. We get what we pay for.

Rick's Rule for this chapter: ***If they want it bad, Give it to them bad!.*** That is exactly what happened to investors at the end of the 90's.

Yellow Dogs and Fruit Flies

They wanted it bad, they were willing to accept investing in companies with little or no visible means of support in order to get rich quick. They got it bad all right. Remember, The best things in life are free, No wonder I'm so happy!

Now our economy is back in full recovery. Interest rates have been at historical lows for nearly three years, fueling a real recovery in the high end market. Housing starts are up, Big ticket sales are up, and a full fledge recovery has begun. As I said earlier, two quarters of significant growth in the job market have taken place. The rhetoric on the left says out sourcing is killing the recovery, nothing could be farther from the truth. The creation of jobs is a lag indicator of economic growth. That is why we are just now seeing the beginnings of job growth. It should only get better from here.

A few weeks ago (before the latest job figures were in), I had several liberal friends who were belaboring the Job loss that was being touted by Democratic Presidential contenders. They all were talking about how terrible the job picture was, and how unemployment was going to kill the economic recovery. I ask them (6 of them), a simple question. I said who do you know, and be specific, that is out of work, who wants a job. I don't want to know who wants to be a CEO but has no training or education, but tell me who do you know that is out of work and wants a real job that they are qualified to do, and I will find them a job today! Not maybe, but unequivocally, because I know employers who are looking to hire today! Not one name, of one person, who was out of work was forthcoming. Out of 6 people, all who were belaboring how terrible it was that so many had no job, not one person could they name.

I'm afraid I didn't cut them much slack. I shamed them for listening to sound bights from candidates and their media, that bore no resemblance to fact. Let's all agree on one thing, our economy is the backbone of the world economy. As goes Wall Street, so goes the rest of the worlds economy. Job growth is a lag indicator of the economy, always has been and always will be, and for good reason. As the economy begins an expansion, it begins as an upturn in demand for goods and services. As that demand expands, the workers who were only getting 35 hours a week and spending the rest of that time on unemployment, begin to work 40 hours a week. Demand has been met, production has increased, with no real increase in unemployment. As demand continues to increase, that same worker may get a little overtime, until finally management decides that it is profitable to hire a new worker.

But as you can see, the upturn in the economy, and the increase in demand for consumer goods and services took place long before a decision to hire more workers was made. In

Yellow Dogs and Fruit Flies

other words the requirement for more workers (higher employment) lags behind the increase in demand, making employment what is called a *Lag* indicator of the economic condition. This is not brain surgery, just common sense, so it has been a source of amazement to me that the media has tried to spin our economic recovery, as a jobless recovery. Now they are having to eat their words AGAIN. It is truly dismaying to me that my party can only find positive news in negative occurances. Why does bad news equate with positive upswings in my parties fortunes? Why do the leaders of my National party find it necessary to continually demean my countries actions in order to have political success. Why oh Why can't the Democratic party do something positive for a change?

Why does my Democratic party have to continually bully and participate in name calling? And more importantly why does the National Media condone that behavior? Ted Kennedy called my president a liar. Why hasn't the media called him to task for that? Al Gore accused my President of betraying this country. Why hasn't the media ask him for proof? John Dean accuses my president of having prior knowledge of September 11th and doing nothing about it. Why has the media allowed him to get by with that?

The so-called bi-partisan 9-11 commission has allowed mean spirited bureaucrats who have been fired for poor job performance to question with impunity my presidents motives. Why has the media allowed them to go unpunished for that? This same commission has found out that one of its own members is personally responsible for problems with the walls thrown up between the CIA and FBI, but yet it has refused to call her to task for it, why does the media not become incensed at this?

Why do we continually allow the media to get by with not just poor reporting, but down right questionable ethics? There is certainly a double standard in this country in how the media deals with issues that is based entirely on politics. Why has the media come out so fiercely this year with a liberal democratic bias? A lot of questions that we all should ask as we turn that dial on our radio or TV.

By the way, as we wonder why the media has betrayed us, I think we have to look long and hard at how we educate our children. I favor parental control of their children's educations. I think certificates that allow parents to take their children out of the public schools in favor of private schools is one way of forcing poor public schools to improve or die. Remember those fruit flies and how the fittest survive, if schools are not doing their job in educating our children they should not be artificially propped up just to meet quotas. I

Yellow Dogs and Fruit Flies

am not in favor of alignment of school districts, or forced busing in order to meet quotas.

I think our children should have a right to hear both sides of an issue, not just the liberal views so many educators preach (yes I said preach not teach). The old adage, that those that can do, those that can't teach, and those that can't teach administer too often holds true. I don't believe that my federal tax dollars should be used to fund education, that is something that should be done by local school boards, without having to pay homage to the NEA, or anyone else in order to get their funding. Would this impact funding level per student? Yes, But funding levels per student is not the problem with education. Throwing more money down the education hole is not going to fix the problem. As schools have become more and more dependent on federal and state support, the education of our children has suffered. We don't need to spend more money on the arts or on making the girls basketball team funded equally with the boy's. Those are not functions of education. If the girl's basketball team can't pay its own way then why should you and I be forced to pay for it?

Being forced to pay for things that individuals have no say in, is one reason that the big labor unions are going the way of the Dodo bird! Union members are sick and tired of paying union dues to National Unions, so they can endorse

Rick Teal

the liberal likes of John Kerry. (It isn't surprising Jumpin' Johnny is trying so desperately to run and hide from his liberal voting record for the past 30 years).

Remember that you get what you pay for, so I think teachers should be tested. For Pete's sake if a teacher is unable to meet minimum standards about the things they are teaching, how can they possibly teach about it? I don't care about ethnic standards, or fairness, I want my money's worth out of my education dollar. If you are a teacher put up or shut up. If you want the job be willing to compete for it just like any other business. As far as teachers being tested, I think voters should be tested also, if you don't have a basic understanding of the issues in a given election, you shouldn't get to vote on them.

I don't think we should be worrying about hurting students feelings by grading their accomplishments. A good dose of stiff competition for grades and further educational opportunities will just welcome them to the real world. As a matter of fact that is one of the most important lessons a school child should be aware of, long before they reach high school. Let's face it, the world isn't fair, and no one is entitled to anything but an opportunity. What you make of it is up to you. You can lead a horse to water but you can't make him drink. The same is true of education, knowledge can't be poured through a funnel.

Teacher's can teach but that doesn't necessarily mean that students will learn. That is totally up to the student. And their parents who anymore are too often absent completely in the education process. Attending all the High School Home Games, doesn't make you pro-education, only a sports fan!

And another thing, Parents, if your child can't read, or do simple math, that is not just his teacher's fault. The blame lies squarely with you too! If your child refuses to learn, shame on you for not getting tough. If your child's school or teachers do a poor job, shame on you for not firing them. Take responsibility for your child's education, and make them aware that you are taking personal responsibility, and will not accept anything but success.

The only way we are ever going to solve our national crises in education, is by taking personal responsibility. Quit being so willing to abdicate your personal responsibility to the government. Not just for the sake of your children's education, but also for the sake of your parents nursing care, paying your doctor, and so many of the other duties that citizens took responsibility for 50 years ago, that today we want to hire the government to do for us!

Our medical costs are soaring for many reasons, not the least of which is our innate unwillingness to pull out our billfolds and pay the doctor ourselves. Instead we try to hire the government or an insurance company to do it for us and then complain about the additional costs.

Chapter 5
What has happened to my Democratic Party

Reader's Cramp Relief: *A Democratic colleague and I stopped at a cross walk in Washington D.C. where a buzzer (one that meets the requirements of the Americans with Disabilities Act) sounds when it is safe to cross the street. As we were crossing, she asked me what that noise was, and I explained that it was so blind people would know when the light had turned red. She looked horrified and asked "What on earth are blind people doing driving?"*

As a member of the silent majority, I realize I have the right to remain silent, but in light of all that is happening today I just can't continue to do so. For the past ten years or so, as I have matured, and become more experienced/*old,*I am more and more frequently being accused of being a Republican. For the most part I have simply laughed it off and attributed it to my conservative upbringing and the inability of most yellow dog democrats to distinguish between a thinking

Rick Teal

democrat who disagrees with our party because of the extreme positions it has been taking for the past ten to twenty years, and their unwillingness to think for themselves. For the most part they are (I attribute it to laziness), willing to be led in directions they don't even recognize because they will not put out the effort or take the time to educate themselves on the issues. As I stated in the last chapter, voters should have to take a test before they get to pull the lever. If you recognize yourself here (and listening to sound bite news broadcasts isn't education), shame on you.

After thinking about this situation for many years, I keep asking myself, when did my party leave me? Who took it? Why did they take it? What did they want it for? And How did I (and the rest of you good conservative democrats) let this happen? Let me respond to this one step at a time. WHEN I think can be answered only if we look back nearly a hundred years. This one question, would be a topic for an entire book, so I will try to be brief and do not intend to factually prove a point, I am only making a statement based on my own observation.

Woodrow Wilson and his dream of a League of Nations, nearly killed the democratic party after WWI. The US economy boomed during the twenties though and the rest of the world was an entire Ocean away, so out of sight out of mind. The Crash in twenty nine, gave the Democrats

Yellow Dogs and Fruit Flies

an opportunity to save this country, which they did very effectively. The Democratic party also led us to victory over the forces of evil during the continuation of WWI which we called WWII. During the Fifties, the democratic party, my party, lost its way I believe. After nearly a quarter century of shoo in elections for Democratic Presidents, Dwight Eisenhower did a most effective job of leading our nation in it's (and the rest of the world's) post war recovery efforts.

So I feel it was during this time that National Democratic leaders began leaning more and more to the left, and finally clutched on the idea that would mold what has been a nearly 40 year sojourn to the left for my party. So when the party changed I believe can be established as the late 50's or early 60's. President Kennedy (and I hereby resolve not to become embroiled in a who assassinated Kennedy expose') was I believe the very last of the Nationally elected conservative democrats. One of his very first actions was to cut taxes, as he realized that is what would drive economic recovery. He was strong on defense and ready to take us to war if the Russians didn't back down in Cuba. He was a strong, forceful, charismatic leader whom I believe was perceived by other nationally prominent democrats, to be a dangerous threat and a detriment to the future of the democratic party as *they* had determined it to be. I think that during the 1960 presidential primary, that deals were made that forced Kennedy to accept Lyndon Johnson as his running mate, and that the rest is history. After Kennedy was assassinated, the Democrats took a definite left turn with Johnson's Great Society.

So When did it turn left? The early 60's, Who turned it? That venerable Texan Lyndon B. Johnson. The most powerful man in the Democratic party at that time, but a man that was virtually unelectable on his own as president. Now let's think about why they took it, and in order to answer that we also have to consider what they wanted it for. Why would the Democratic National Committee take such a resolute turn to the left? In order to consider this, we have to remember that they had been resoundingly defeated in the past two national elections, by a War Hero that controlled the hearts and minds (and imaginations) of the country. While they had been able to elect a president in 1960, it was a president in the same conservative mold, that made no guarantee of future successes against a conservative Republican party that appealed to so much of the conservative democratic base. We were filled with National Pride but also fear of the nuclear war scenario. That was the appeal that Kennedy had, a strong leader on National Defense to follow up the accomplishments of Dwight Eisenhower. So it became an either, or scenario for the National Democratic party. It either had to continue as the war fighting, tax cutting party that had to compete with the Republican party that also believed in

Yellow Dogs and Fruit Flies

strong defense and low taxes. It meant that to continue on that road would mean 50% of the time and 50% of the government would be all that the Democrats could reasonably expect to control at any given time. As at this time both parties goals and expectations were pretty well middle of the road, as were the political ideals of the average American and I believe they still are.

This was unacceptable to the Democrats in control of the party as it would mean sharing power. It was also at a time when a new direction was being taken by many of the youth in America, the feel good generation was here, I was one. Young adults in the late 60's and early 70's were fed up with War (Viet Nam), and with old men running the country. This generation had never known hard times (economically), the war they had fought was not winable, and they were not willing to continue allowing old men with tired ideas to continue leading them. They (we) were ripe for the picking. After all, we were 18 to 25 years old, knew it all and fully expected to live forever.

So it was then that the Democratic National Committee (DNC) was able to hijack my party. How did they do it? They appealed to our (my and your) GREED and LAZINESS. They said don't worry, just sit back and vote for us and we'll see to it that your are taken care of. You don't need to think, we'll take care of that for you! And the devious diabolical part of their plan was not only to capture our imaginations with their socialistic ideals, but to also enslave us to the extent that we would never be able to say no again! At least not until it was too late, until our country had given program entitlements to enough voters that 51% of the vote would be available to the party that controlled the entitlements. Whether it is seniors eating in Older Americans Act Nutrition sites, or environmentalists needing to save the spotted owl, enough control of our government has to be controlled by voters whose cups are half empty, instead of half full. That's how my party became the party of the half empty cup.

How can a free society be enslaved? How can we be induced to give up our freedoms? Really it was quite simple, and the DNC was masterful in implementing its plot over the long term. Looking back I can only appreciate the political skill involved in this hijacking. Quite simple indeed, ***you need only make 51% of the voting public dependent on government for its livelihood in order to make government untouchable (and unstoppable) by the masses.*** So Lyndon Baines and his Great Society, set about making benefits (entitlements as we still call them today) available to the masses. The Older Americans Act is a perfect example (and also one with which I am very familiar). The theory was simple, and the implementation was even simpler. Provide service programs that are easily defendable as needed (ie. Feeding old folks will lengthen their lives and

Yellow Dogs and Fruit Flies

allow them to live a more independent life). In reality though it makes a certain percentage of the population dependent (if not dependent then certainly agreeable) to more government that can and will give them entitlement to more goods and services. Just vote democratic, it's free, we'll make the government support you!

So over the course of the past 40 years, the movement to the left of the democratic party has been fueled by collecting more taxes (a higher percentage of your and my income), in order to provide more entitlements to more programs for more people, in order to maintain the 51% of the voting public dependent on those services. The part of the theory that doesn't hold water though is beginning to be felt however. So many of us that don't need or want the services, who refuse to become dependent on the system, or who will not (or cannot) learn to work the system to our advantage, have started to see the light. Less taxation means I have more control over my own life. I do not require governments intervention in my life. I am perfectly able to think for myself, and will never allow some bureaucrat to do my thinking for me. It is high time we realized that paying the doctor ourselves when we were sick as our parents did, is much cheaper than hiring the insurance companies (private or government) to do it for us.

Rick Teal

I remember when as a member of a Labor Union working in my home town, I had the best medical benefits in the world. When I or a member of my family did have to go to the doctor, I paid nothing out of pocket. I can even remember fellow union members who would schedule back surgery just before labor negotiations, so they could be receiving their medical payments while we were on strike. I recall other members of my community resenting the fact that medical attention cost me literally nothing. That desire of everyone to have (for all practical purposes) free medical care, has created the situation we find ourselves in today. Now when I go to the doctor for a checkup, I pay a co-pay that is as much as the entire doctors call cost 30 years ago. My co-pay for my prescriptions is as high now as the prescription was 30 years ago.

Why has this happened? Next time your at your doctors office, look around at how many receptionist and bill collectors he has to hire in order to do business, In order for him to keep the records required by governmental regulation, in order for him to get paid for Medicare and Medicaid claims. We have created this monster because we wanted to go to the Doctor free. Well we got what we wanted to pay for didn't we.

Much as the pyramid get rich schemes of the 60's and 70's (Amway is one), collapsed of their own weight, so will the effects of more and

Yellow Dogs and Fruit Flies

more endless government spending programs to enslave the masses eventually cave in from the sheer expense of it. We are already feeling that enormous weight bearing down on future generations. Where as many as 200 workers supported the first participants in Social Security, by 2020 only 2-3 workers will have to support that same burden of a retiree on their backs. I am all for seeing to it that Senior Citizens are fed well and remain independent, but I don't feel that the Federal government should handle this as an entitlement. This is something (as is education) that should be provided by local populations for the local senior citizens or their children. The real fallacy that so many conservatives have finally recognized is: That it is ridiculous to collect a dollar in federal taxes, to send to Washington D.C. in the hopes of getting a quarter back with which to feed senior citizens. Let's give the dollar back to the federal taxpayer, collect a half dollar from the local taxpayer, cut out the middleman and provide twice the level of service for half as much money!

Rick's Lesson for this chapter: You can't hire the government to make people be good to each other! This whole fiasco began in the 60's to promote a better life for all Americans, but the price is too high. It is high time that we quit trying to hire the government to force us as individuals to do the right thing. It is high time that we all begin again to take personal responsibility for our actions (and inactions). If the children of your town need better education, or the seniors of your city require better services, take action yourself, don't beg Uncle Sam to do it for you, It Ain't his Job! ***And more importantly, You and I can't afford to hire him to do it!!!***

People ask what has happened to the Democratic Party, I think this is the answer, they have betrayed their base. By trying to appeal to everyone, by trying to be the answer for all minority groups, they have lost their appeal to their base voters. They have to try and appeal to environmental groups, who have a completely different (very costly) set of priorities than say meet the interests of the Hispanic vote. Too many groups with varying priorities.

The IMPOSSIBLE CONUNDRUM:

How did we get started down this road? I think again we have to look back to the first half of the 20th century. I don't mean to impugn the right of minorities or women to vote. That is not my intent, but the very amendment to the constitution that gave them the right to vote (a good case for care when proposing to amend it), also gave universal suffrage to those who do not pay taxes. Anytime you allow those who do nothing to support a democratically formed government a voice in how that government operates, I think it is clear that *give me more* will become their battle cry.

Yellow Dogs and Fruit Flies

It is not the right of an American to *have* things, it is the right of an American to provide things for themselves.

Equality is not guaranteed under our constitution, that is a myth that has been sold to America by the Democratic party (sad but true). Americans are guaranteed an equal opportunity, not equality. Let's face it, a person who is disabled (let's say blindness) will never be equal to a sighted person. But they can still have an equal opportunity, they just don't have the same physical abilities with which to take advantage of that opportunity. It is a sad truth, but never the less a truth. Let's not forget the Fruit Fly, it is an undeniable Law of God that the fittest survive, and no matter how much we would like that to be otherwise, God in his infinite wisdom, has determined it as a universal law that we would be wise to remember. I am sick of being politically correct, it is high time we quit hating the rich and pitying the poor, neither deserve it.

It is maddening to me to hear so many members of our party espouse very conservative view points, and then continue to vote for extremely liberal candidates, simply because they have a (D) next to their name on the ballot. On issues ranging from forced busing in the 60's in order to meet quotas, to Tax Cuts in the 80's, these conservative views have been politicized. More often than not the side of conservative candidates (usually Republicans

Rick Teal

but not always), have been spun out of control by mass media (let's call them Walter Cronkite) sound bites. This spin that supports the liberal view point has become a basic position of the national media. Too many conservative democrats vote for liberal candidates because they are unable (or too lazy) to research the issues for themselves and find out. If you read this and recognize yourself, then here again, shame on you. Understand it for what it is and from this day forward vow to be a thinking democrat instead of a Yellow Dog Democrat! Only when we make the leadership of the democratic party aware that they will no longer be allowed to hijack our party for their liberal viewpoints that the majority of democrats don't believe in, will we be able to take *our party* back.

Chapter 6
Who am I to Talk?

Readers Cramp Relief: <u>I work with a lady who plugged her power strip back into itself, and for the life of her couldn't understand why in world her computer system still wouldn't turn on!</u>

I am an American, an Oklahoman, and a Democrat. I am a retired 1SG in the Oklahoma Army National Guard. I am a father of two (son and daughter) and grand father of (at this writing), 3. I am divorced and now remarried. I am currently Director of a small Senior Citizens Services program, a non-profit, that operates in 3 counties of NE Oklahoma. Over 1200 Senior Citizens have lunch with my program everyday, and we also provide other services for seniors, but more of the commercial later.

I deal daily with our governmental bureaucracy, so I think I have a better than average understanding of how and why it works (and often times doesn't). I am also a person who reads, and hopefully understands at least part of what I read. I am becoming more cynical each year, as I see

Rick Teal

more and more misuse of governmental powers. For example I do not believe that government has my best interests at heart. I have seen too many instances, when the primary force driving this bureaucracy to move, is inertia. Once it starts you can't stop it, and if it should stop it may never move again!

My role as director of the program is to write grants (beg), initiate service programs, hire good staff to run them and accomplish our goals and objectives, and then get out of the way and let them. One of my favorite militarisms of all times is *"Lead, Follow, or Get the Hell out of the Way!"* I am a firm believer in practicing what I preach. I have been blessed with great employees, and I try very hard not to micro-manage. I want to be there when and if they require my assistance, and I don't mind being the bad guy when they need someone to blame things on either. Goes with the territory. I have been president of my state association of Nutrition Service providers for several years, and can attest to how frustrating it is when our state agency bureaucrats priorities of agency power collide with providing adequate services for senior citizens.

I have been on both ends of good and bad ideas, and can tell you for certain that what is right and wrong has very little to do with what actually takes place. The right way, the wrong way, and the Governments way. **I have adopted this as**

Yellow Dogs and Fruit Flies

Rick's Lesson for Chapter 6: The Right Way, The Wrong Way, and the Government Way. (as adapted from the World War II GI's right way, wrong way and army way). A couple of examples: Beginning with the TVA back in the 30's the Rural Electric Cooperatives were started and subsidized by the government in order to provide electrical power across America. HELLO, I think America is certainly electrified, so why are the American taxpayers still subsidizing REC's. Often times their main purpose is to stifle free competition with other power companies. Our electrical grid is to sensitive (potential terrorist targets), to continue subsidizing an out dated bureaucracy to operate in it. I am not saying that Rural Electric Coops don't have a role to play, I am merely pointing out that this is an outmoded bureaucratic model, that needs to be modernized or forced to compete without tax support. If we are going to subsidize electrification, let's make it more secure from terrorist attack, or at the very least update the infrastructure that makes it so vulnerable.

Another governmental bureaucracy that needs to be modernized or done away with is the USDA. It was formed in the 30's to subsidize the farmer, and help us through the depression by governmental oversight of the food supply. HELLO why are we still involved as a government in something out of date for 50 years??

Rick Teal

Let's face it, it has become the highest priority for every governmental department to continue as a department. An administrator's primary goal is to keep their job, not carryout the work of their department. Increasing the amount of money it takes to operate their agency is the priority of most administrators. I have yet to hear an administrator brag about reducing his agencies budget. I have heard a lot of complaining when it happens, but never have I heard a bureaucrat that was proud of spending less money. I have heard them say they are saving the taxpayers money by spending more, and can even, as an administrator myself, sell you one about my program, but that don't necessarily make it so. I'll take it up later as a demonstration of my powers of persuasion, you don't have to be the brightest bulb in the chandelier to convince 51% of the people of anything at any given time. Just ask any politician!

If our government truly has our best interests in mind, shouldn't it be looking out for the best buy it can get us in every instance?? Wouldn't it reinvent itself in order to continually offer what was needed to who needed it when it was needed. Instead of recruiting clients for existing programs, shouldn't we be forming programs to fit the needs of the people who need them? Why are we so intent on driving square pegs into round holes? Can't we cut through so much government red tape and make people our focus again instead of government? So much of what our government

Yellow Dogs and Fruit Flies

does is begun to fill a basic need of the people, but most often, by the time the bureaucracy can work the need has changed and is no longer valid. Why can't we stop it or at least change its direction. The answer is we can, but only if those citizens who are paying for government, have the final say in what that government is about. One more time: If you don't pay taxes, you should not be allowed a voice in how they are spent! Only tax payers should be allowed to vote, and then only if they are informed as to what the real issues are.

I have been accused of being a Republican, I am not, I am a Conservative Thinking Democrat. Unfortunately there aren't very many of us left. I am not a Yellow Dog Democrat, that is, one that punches a straight party ticket regardless of the candidates with no conscious thought. *The expression Yellow Dog Democrat was coined to express the opinion of so many in the 30's that they would vote for a yellow dog before they would vote Republican!* I believe that voting is a right, a privliege, but most of all a duty. I believe that to vote without making every effort to educate yourself on the issues is un-American. I would support testing on the issues of all voters, before they enter the booth. The only thing worse than not voting, is voting without thought. It is every citizens duty to not only vote, but to be an informed voter. To be informed about the issues, and that means hearing both sides of the issue and making a judgment based on informed opinion (yours not

Rick Teal

someone else's). It ain't easy being a thinking person, but is required in order to do your patriotic duty as a citizen.

I seldom if ever agree with everything another person says. As a matter of fact I don't recall ever agreeing with anyone, or anything, 100%. I take pride in thinking things through for myself, and coming to my own conclusions, and mistrust anyone who encourages me to take their opinion as my own. I have never met another human being, who I so respected and trusted, that I would abdicate by own decision making responsibility in favor of theirs. *However I do know many people whom I believe should allow me to do all of their decision making! Which I would happily do. Not really conceit, just a healthy dose of self respect. I do study the issues at length and many people could benefit greatly from my knowledge, so read on and become politically educated.*

It is difficult for me to even conceptualize any individual being so lazy or unsure of themselves, that they would allow someone else to do their thinking for them. I have known and I am sure you have too, many people who would rather have someone else do their thinking for them than to take the time and make the effort to discover for themselves. *And as I said I will be more than happy to do their thinking for them.*

Yellow Dogs and Fruit Flies

Nothing so infuriates me, as for someone to argue a point, having absolutely no personal knowledge of what they say, that they are only parroting a sound bite they heard on the 6 o'clock news, totally accepting it as gospel, and never questioning the source. No little wonder that the Media has become so powerful, they can and regularly do sell ice to Eskimos, and so many in their audience buy without thinking about the price, or whether the Frigidaire will hold it all.

I am an American, I am an Oklahoman, and I am a Democrat:

But I will not support a national party that promotes better benefits for the poor than for the working middle class and requires the middle class to pay for them. A national party that refuses to even acknowledge the wishes of the majority.

I am an American, I am an Oklahoman, and I am a Democrat:

But I will not support a national party that promotes the Appeasement of Terrorists.

I am an American, I am an Oklahoman, and I am a Democrat:

But I will not support a national party willing to accept illegal immigration by providing education, medical benefits, and income support for illegal immigrants.

I am an American, I am an Oklahoman, and I am a Democrat:

But I will not support rhetoric currently being fed by a national party that is more interested in Europeans liking us, than in confronting the terrorists who have killed us.

I am an American, I am an Oklahoman, and I am a Democrat:

But I am a conservative also. That is allowed, just because you are a democrat, does not mean that you have to change your values to fit a national party that has moved so far to the left that it no longer represents my values.

I am an American, I am an Oklahoman, and I am a Democrat:

But I will not support a national party that actively uses partisan political tricks to block the appointment of conservatives as Judges, just because they are conservative.

I am an American, I am an Oklahoman, and I am a Democrat:

But I will not support a national party that advocates for the rights of gays to marry. Or for the rights of snail darters over that of Americans.

I am an American, I am an Oklahoman, and I am a Democrat:

But I will not support a national party who has to cater to Special interests, in order to control enough votes to win a national election. A national party that has to buy votes. That has to promise support and services to special interest groups, in order to control enough votes to win. A party that no longer has a real political base in our society because it governs by appealing to special interests rather than to real people. That has to sell its soul to those interests in order to maintain its political power.

I am an American, I am an Oklahoman, and I am a Democrat:

But I will not support a national party that needs to make 51% of the population dependent upon government for its very lively-hood. Such a party cannot represent the priorities of a free, self-dependent society. The other 49% who work, pay taxes, buy homes, and otherwise support our economy, should not be burdened with the 51% who do not.

Rick Teal

I am an American, I am an Oklahoman, and I am a Democrat,

But I will not vote for a candidate who would cut and run from Iraq, rather than support our troops there. Who would appease terrorists in order to please Europeans.

I am an American, I am an Oklahoman, and I am a Democrat,

But I will not vote for a candidate who changes his mind more often than his underwear.

I am an American, I am an Oklahoman, and I am a Democrat:

But I will not vote for a candidate who has the most liberal voting record in Congress. And does not represent or hold dear the ideals of a conservative democrat.

I am an American, I am an Oklahoman, and I am a Democrat:

But I will not vote for a candidate who says he has the interests of the poor and downtrodden at heart, but who has no concept of how they live.

Yellow Dogs and Fruit Flies

I am an American, I am an Oklahoman, and I am a Democrat:

But I will not vote for a candidate who has belonged to an organization (Vietnam Veterans against the War), who in the 1970's actually discussed killing Members of Congress who were pro war and disagreed with their views.

I am an American, I am an Oklahoman, and I am a Democrat:

But I will not vote for a candidate who has based his entire political life on One World Government. Who believes that the only way to deal with the world is to weaken the United States of America, so that we are no longer a threat to the rest of the World.

A man that believes that we should have the blessings of Kofi Anon and the United Nations before we protect ourselves.

I am an American, I am an Oklahoman, and I am a Democrat:

But I will not vote for a man who believes that Americans should not be allowed to own and bear arms.

Rick Teal

I am an American, I am an Oklahoman, and I am a Democrat:

But I will not vote for a man who believes that the opinions of European leaders (those whose views are at odds with what is best for a strong America) are more important than mine.

I am an American, I am an Oklahoman, and I am a Democrat:

But I will not vote for a candidate who actually introduced a bill in 1995 that would have emasculated our intelligence and defense capabilities even more than they were, in order to spend a ***Peace Dividend.*** A man who actually believed that we no longer needed the CIA, Who has voted against every major new weapons system that we are using today to win the war on terror. How can a person with no more foresight than that hope to lead the most powerful nation in the world?

I'll tell you, he doesn't intend to. He believes that we should so weaken ourselves, that we would have to ask for protection from the UN just like everyone else does. Don't you see? That is the only way that those who believe in one world government can ever accept the United States into the fold of the rest of the World, is to bring us down to their level. The rest of the world will not accept our views of one world government, and as long as we are the only Super Power, we stand in the way of that Goal.

I am an American, I am an Oklahoman, and I am a Democrat:

But I will not vote for a candidate regardless of party affiliation that condones and uses, to his political advantage, the Liberally biased Mass Media.

I am an American, I am an Oklahoman, and I am a Democrat:

But I will not vote for a candidate that travels in the same crowds as traitors like Hanoi Jane Fonda.

I Believe that all men are born with inalienable rights to the same protections and requirements of our government. While we all have the same rights to life, liberty, and the pursuit of happiness, as guranteed by our Constitution, only GOD can make us EQUAL, and for reasons known only to Him, we are not now, never have been, and probably, at least until judgment, day never will be.

I believe I should be able to Pledge Allegiance to my Flag with the words under GOD intact. I think my money, that the government is so anxious to take, should have the words in God We Trust on it. I believe that praying to God in school is perfectly alright, but that preaching Gay rights isn't.

I believe I should be able to Pray to my God when and where I want to. I do not believe that making politically correct statements should be the focus of my every word. I will speak what I believe to be is true, if you disagree fine, you also have a right to speak what you believe, but you do not have the right to restrict or abridge my right to free speech because it will make you feel bad, or less of an American. Get a life, if you cannot defend your beliefs logically, perhaps there is a problem with your beliefs

I also believe that if you don't pay taxes or otherwise support our government, you shouldn't have a say in how it is run, or what it's priorities are. As we talked about earlier, it has only been since the passage of the universal suffrage amendment to the Constitution, that we have seen the huge shift to the left of my National Party.

I will never believe as so many national leaders of my party have, in a one world government, such as the United Nations, or before that the League of Nations. I do not agree with everything that George Bush has done since his election in fact I disagree vehemently on many issues, but I thank God everyday that he has been our leader

Yellow Dogs and Fruit Flies

this past 4 years instead of Al Gore. I thank God that for the first time in many years we have Adult leadership, that recognizes the important things and wastes no time on the irrelevant. I only regret, that it was not my party that has been able to make these things possible.

Chapter 7
The Rest of the Story

Readers Cramp Relief: *As director of a food service program, I regularly attend Food Shows. At a banquet after one of these affairs, while going to the buffet line, I asked the lady serving in the salad area for minimal lettuce. She looked me right in the eye and apologized as she explained that they only had iceberg lettuce.*

As I promised in the last chapter, I will now explain how to sell ice to Eskimos, or more to the point, how to sell a politician on spending **your tax** money on my programs.

Over the past 35 years in the military and now as a program director, I have had some considerable experience in the business of writing grants, obtaining funding for new programs, and generally selling politicians local, state, and federal, on supporting my programs. All in all Services for Seniors is an easily salable program, as it does help so many people. Providing meals for frail elderly, is a good thing to do. It makes people feel good to be able to contribute to that cause.

Yellow Dogs and Fruit Flies

Especially if it costs them nothing personally to do it. The whole theory of government funding for programs, is that it is something we do collectively as a society, not as individuals. That way we don't feel the pain so much.

This is off the subject, but I have found that most liberals are pretty stingy with their own money. They are usually poor tippers in restaurants, and not generous givers to charities. They are however very free with money when it belongs to someone else. Maybe a way to assuage their guilt feelings for personal stinginess. While they don't want to tip a waitress, they do want to try and raise their minimum wage with someone else's money. Alright, back to the subject of this chapter.

In fact the only programs easier to sell than services for seniors, are services for children. The theory is that everyone, including politicians, has been a child but most of us have yet to be old (although I am rapidly approaching it). It is relatively easy to sell a politician on doing something that most of his constituents feels is a good thing to do. In fact, that is something that most good politicians will use in a re-election campaign. I can convince almost anyone, because it is true, that to feed a person one meal a day and by doing so keep them in their home, will save literally thousands of dollars. Let's face it, extended Nursing Home Care for seniors is not only undesirable for most senior citizens who don't want to lose their independence, but it is the most costly way to care for them. Keeping a senior at home as long as is possible, is better for all concerned. That can't be argued. I regularly make the statement to my staff, that when a senior citizen dies in their own bed, in their own home, as a recipient of our services, it only attests to the fact that we are doing a good job. We have done what we are supposed to do, what the taxpayers are hiring us to do.

The fallacy of course is the expense. Just because it saves tax dollars to keep people at home, doesn't mean the way we are doing it in the most cost effective way. **Case in point**: The Older Americans Act in Oklahoma averages statewide between $4.50 and $6.00 per meal. Hidden in that cost, is administration of a federal grant. A good program will have to spend 8-10% on administration to meet requirements of the award., some not so good programs may spend a much higher percentage.), Costs of monitoring successes and failures, expenses incurred in client finding, and generally meeting many requirements that have little if anything to do with services or meal/delivery costs. Often times as much as 30-50% of the total cost of the services are hidden non-service costs imposed as mandates of the federally granted funds. Many hidden agendas, can be found. Requirements to hire a dietician even though we already have literally thousands of menus written. Requirements to provide set hours of operation even when not necessary.

Yellow Dogs and Fruit Flies

Requirements to meet often times ridiculous standards for hiring, advertising, salary, etc. that only force the cost of service to be much higher than it should.

These are all things that preclude good management at the local level. These are also things that can be found in all programs sponsored by and responsible to the Federal governments bureaucratic oversight. "***Be careful what you ask for, you might get it.***" That's **Rick's lesson for this chapter.** Often times when we request funding assistance from the Federal bureaucracy in building a building, or running a program, the immediate ease of gaining the funding we need out weighs the long term vision of what and how we want to operate. We in a cense sell our soul to the Devil or should I say sell our program to the government.

My program contracts annually to provide meals for other funding sources, which we are often able to do for less than half what that same meal paid for by the Older Americans Act costs. Yet it is a great program, yes it does a great deal of good for seniors, yes it allows seniors to remain independent and healthy later in life, but we are often forced to spend nearly half of the cost of the program on superfluous costs that could better be spent on additional services. One of my favorite expressions is *"if it aint broke don't fix it"* but conversely if it is we should don't you think?

Rick Teal

I have not even begun to talk about the costs associated with operation of Federal and State bureaucracies for the purpose of funding and monitoring such programs. 15-25% (probably a low estimate) of the total cost of Older Americans Act services is spent before it ever reaches the service provider level. And then the actual cost of the service is still double what a locally funded service will cost. Here in Oklahoma, we have what are known as independent senior centers, often times they operate with little paid staff and locally supported operating budgets. Such programs as this are able to provide that $6 dollar meal for $2.50-$3.00 or even less.

Now as taxpayers you need to realize that you get what you pay for. Those programs may not provide as balanced a diet, because they want fried chicken with mashed potatoes and gravy twice a week. They may not serve milk everyday, they probably won't always provide a 3rd of the RDA, but they will feed senior citizens for less than half what a federally subsidized program costs. Just like the military decision of whether you want to pay for a standing army or a reserve army, it depends on your viewpoint. Be careful what you ask for you might get it.

In-Home Services for Seniors are a bargain when compared to Extended Stay Nursing Home Care. While they needn't cost per unit what we currently spend. But remember that if you just cut

Yellow Dogs and Fruit Flies

funding and not the bureaucracy that operates it, you will cut services, because no self serving bureaucracy is going to do away with bureaucrats in order to maintain levels of services. In fact those very bureaucrats whose job it is to see that the services are provided, may feel threatened and coerce service providers into cutting services in order to bring pressure on the politicians being asked to make hard choices during times of funding crisis. That is the fallacy of hiring government to make us do good for one another. The first ones we are going to do good for are the bureaucrats the government hires to run the program. Remember we are the government! You don't have to be the sharpest knife in the drawer to cut through the logic in that. I sometimes think the American taxpayer/voter was left on the tilt-a-whirl too long as a child.

Now here me, when you take that approach, and you lose governmental over sight of programs you have to accept what you pay for. You, we have to be willing to accept responsibility for operations of services ourselves, at the local level. If you are one of those that want to hire the government to do your job, that is what it costs. Whether it is meals for senior citizens, or insurance coverage for low income recipients (Medicaid), or any of a thousand other services that we have over the past 40 years hired the government to provide for us, we are paying an exorbitant fee for it. I often times hear local seniors lament what the *government* makes them do to get their subsidies and services. I sometimes want to scream, be careful what you ask for, you might get it. So often we lose sight of the fact that local control means local funding. If you want full control of the programs in your community, to be based in your community, don't hire the federal government to tell you how to run it. More often than not, they won't have a clue what is best for your community.

By looking at this analogy of senior citizens service programs, it can be plainly seen that to reduce the costs, ***do it yourself***. Don't escape back to hiring the government to make you do what's right, we can't afford it. Save that 15-25% spent on buying Federal oversight of how your programs are run. That way you do it totally with local control, (and if you don't like it the way it is, you can change it locally also). By total control locally, you can also provide just the services your community needs, in the form in which it wants it, with no intervention from the *Feds.* This can also mean an additional savings of 40-50% of the total costs of the program, simply by changing and accepting responsibility for those changes of things you provide locally.

I have had experience with State and Federal monitors coming into a facility and writing us up for running a site or holding a function, that is counter to State or Federal guidelines, regardless of how petty, they need to justify their existence.

Yellow Dogs and Fruit Flies

I have also been told that we could request a waiver for a mandated policy or requirement, if it were something that could be defended. So we have a case where we as taxpayers send money to Washington D.C. to pay for services in our community, and then have to ask for permission (that's what a waiver amounts to), to provide the services in a manner that fits the requirements of local senior citizens. It certainly seems an upside down operation to me. Easily you can provide the same or even better service for less than half what it costs now as a federal program. That means collecting the costs locally, spending them locally, and accepting responsibility for what take's place <u>(or more importantly what doesn't take place)</u> locally.

Here again, as Director of a program that depends on Federal, State, and Local governmental subsidies, there is a more cost effective way of providing services. But don't throw the dishes out with the dish water. The services are critical to our society, we are just spending more on them than we need to. Before we can begin to fund programs at the local level, we must quit taxing for them at the Federal level. A big step to take! And one that will be resisted heartily by all levels of our bureaucracy that currently funds them.

I have seen, generally in more urban settings, how some programs have been able to resist taking those governmental subsidies, and begun

Rick Teal

running their programs totally with local funds. The savings is dramatic.

Remember the Fruit Fly and don't vote yourself into becoming a candidate for Natural Selection, by voting the Yellow Dog Democrat straight party line. Discriminate freely when you go to the voting booth and select the candidate regardless of party affiliation that most nearly reflects your ideas. And for Pete's sake think about it and educate yourself before you pull that lever, punch that ballot, or other wise make your mark.

By the way, just as a point of reference, I feel much safer letting a machine with no political affiliation count my vote. Thanks for reading my book, There will be a test, and our grade depends on how well we mark that next ballot.

Chapter 8
The Real of the Rest of the Story

Reader's Cramp Relief: *The first thing to do when you find yourself in a hole, is to quit digging!*

I have talked a great deal so far about what is wrong, and what I feel needs to take place as an immediate fix for immediate problems, ie. Terrorism. In this final chapter I want to talk about some solutions to long term problems in our country and society.

Perceived problems within our military are not problems that can't be dealt with on an individual basis. No systemic solutions are required. Case in point is the violations that took place in Abu-Grahib prison in Iraq. These happened as aberrations to our policy, and were not, nor have they ever been condoned. In fact, the system within the Military itself, already in place, is handling them. Punishing the guilty and hopefully rewarding those that had the courage to blow the whistle on their comrades who were participating in these acts is sufficient.

Let's not forget that these acts, no matter how perverse, pale into the background when compared to the real atrocities being perpetrated by the Islamic Jihadists that pervade the middle east. It is the governments of the middle east that fail to condemn these acts, it is the media worldwide that fails to distinguish the difference, and *it is this nations leaders of the Democratic National Committee, and some Democratic Senators (Kennedy comes to mind) that should be held to account.* Held to account for condoning and accepting as our fault the acts of these same Islamic fundamentalists who are the enemy combatants of the entire Free World.

I can understand the Middle East governments attitudes, they will not be able to retain power without the Terrorists. The Media in that part of the World is controlled by those same governments who rely on Terrorism to get their way, but the Media in this country, and the Leaders of my Democratic party have no excuse. Their actions are unconscionable and wrong. They are purposely politicizing for purely partisan gains this War on Terror.

Let's look at our culture compared to the Islamic Culture. While we investigate the abuses of our army, while we are prepared to punish

Yellow Dogs and Fruit Flies

them for these actions, and even pay money to the victims (perhaps a poor word for the sorry SOB's that were trying to kill us) of these acts. These cowardly Muslims kill civilians who are in their country trying to help them!

Remember this is World War IV. This War is taking place all over the world. In New York, in Maryland and Virginia (Remember Mohammed the sniper), in Bali, in the Philippines all around the World. The vicious murder of an American civilian, by cowardly Muslim radicals, and the total lack of outrage by the Arab World to it, should be evidence that reawakens our resolve to kill them until the last one is dead or incarcerated.

Nuke'um 'til they glow, then drill through the glass to get the oil out. Let's quit giving the Muslim world the benefit of the doubt. Enough is enough, how much proof of duplicity do we need to conclude that we are being attacked by radical, Islamists who are being actively supported by their respective governments that are directly controlled by the Islamic Religios leaders.

You may not want to think about it, but the constant encouragement that these Terrorists have to be receiving from the American Left, and our media borders on treason. It cannot be condoned nor excused, and I am one conservative democrat that is ashamed of the role my party is playing in this war.

Rick Teal

Now that I have gotten that off my chest. I'll get down to the real meat of this chapter: **Long Term Problems need long term solutions.** That's the lesson for this chapter, Band Aids won't work. There are some very real problems in how our government is formed (or I should say has been changed in the last 100 years). These are some very good reasons to exercise great care before amending our Constitution. It may not be perfect, but most of the changes that have taken place since the Bill of Rights, have been politically motivated, short term solutions to long term problems.

As was mentioned a few chapters back, and I won't belabor the point further, is the need to make those individuals (Taxpayers) who support our government totally responsible for its direction. Those that don't support it should not have a say in how it operates or how much money is collected for its support. For that reason, I would support a **National Sales Tax,** in place of our temporary income tax system as administered by the IRS. (Yes this is a temporary tax system put in place to help pay for WWI). As we discussed earlier, the IRS is another one of those huge, bloated, irresponsible, out of control Federal bureaucracies that needs to be done away with. *I wonder if this will result in an AUDIT???*

A simple National Sales tax where everyone who consumes, helps pay his or her own way would

Yellow Dogs and Fruit Flies

make universal suffrage, universally acceptable. Many good methods of implementation have been proposed over the past 25 years. Pick one. The latest makes provisions for exemptions for necessities, which would give a relatively large break to low income citizens, but still mean a huge savings to all (except employees of the IRS and some CPA's).

Next: Repeal the 17th amendment to the Constitution. I was visiting with a friend the other day, and he made the statement that we should get rid of the U.S. Senate. That it was unneeded and in the way of good government. Well I had to disagree with him to the extent that the U.S. Senate (as defined in the constitution) is needed as a check on the House of Representatives. Without it, small states like Oklahoma, would pay taxes so that those large states who can easily control the House, would get all the benefits.

No the answer is to get rid of the 17th amendment. Very few people are aware that the 17th amendment altered the procedure for electing Senators. It was never an intention of our founding father's (for good reasons) for The Senate to be popularly elected. Up until that time, Senators were responsible to state legislatures for their votes, not the voters. It was the original intent, that the Senate be a body that represents the rights of the States. That's why Senators number 2 from each state regardless of population. They are not supposed to be super Representatives of the people. They are supposed to uphold the best interests of the individual states.

I might also mention here, that the same year (1913) that the Senate was changed, is also the same year that the IRS was formed to collect income taxes. It is also interesting, that it was the media (The Hurst newspapers were especially active), that had a big hand in selling this (perpetrating another fraud) to the American people.

It is only after this amendment that we have seen the huge increase in the size of the Federal Bureaucracy. The Senate was a check on the power that could be usurped by the Federal Government, as it effectively gave veto power over the size and scope of Federal government, back to the States in the form of the U.S. Senate.

In summary, until we as a country again begin to act as a nation of States, until we again recognize that collecting taxes at the Federal level through control of individual income, and until we realize that pitting the states against each other in the competition for Federal dollars to support local programs is counter to good government, we will continue on a downward spiral.

Yellow Dogs and Fruit Flies

It is not within the scope of the Federal Government to decide how much local areas spend on education, or helping senior citizens, or any other benefit of citizenship. The Federal Government has no business telling us how much we should or should not spend helping our fellow citizens. These are things that we as Americans are going to have to take personal responsibility for.

We can no longer afford the luxury of burying our heads in the sand and calling on the Federal Government to make us be good to each other. We can no longer expect the Federal government to provide medical care for us, or any of the entitlement programs that have so bloated this government. It is time to take responsibility for it ourselves.

Our government was never intended to be one size fits all. If it is going to get better, it is up to us the voters and taxpayers to decide how, and it's high time we took that decision back from a bureaucracy that no longer remembers what it is there for. We are the government. Let's not forget it. We can't afford to do otherwise.

Rick Teal

Are You a Liberal or Conservative?

You Decide

***Average
American***

Left Right

Liberal *Conservative*

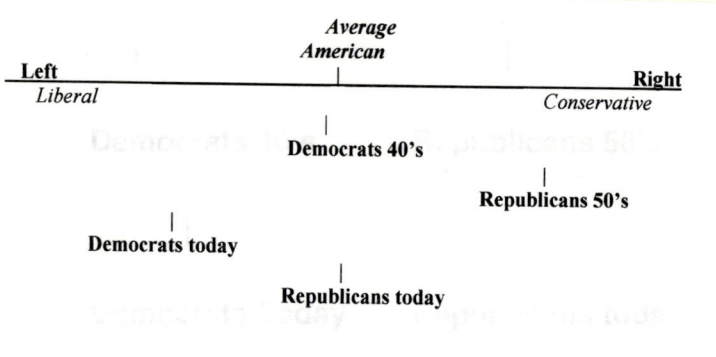

GOD BLESS AMERICA

Rick Teal, Grove, OK

Epilogue

This Election, In this year will be a defining point for not only this country and this year, but also for the World and the 21st Century. I am convinced, that the single most important issue facing our country and the world today is Terrorism! Let's not make the mistake of allowing this country to depend, even become dependent upon the whims of the United Nations. It is imperative that we elect a President, and a Congress this year that will be tough on terror, and be willing to do so unilaterally if necessary. I do not believe my Party's Candidate John Kerry is capable or willing to take that course. In fact he has already stated on countless occasions that he would seek help from the United Nations in dealing with Iraq. That he would refuse to act unilaterally regardless of the situation.

During the entire presidency of Bill Clinton, we buried our heads in the sand. We took no action when we should have. Instead of looking the other way after the 1st bombing of the World Trade Center, the bombing of the Marine Corp barracks in Lebanon, the Korean debacle that Jimmy Carter negotiated for us, the bombing of the Cole, and any of a half dozen other terrorist acts, we should have taken action then. If we had, we would not be in the state we find ourselves today. Why did we not follow up on offers by Sudan to hand over Bin Laden in 1997?

Why were we not more proactive in taking care of the CIA and FBI during the 90's? These are all head in the sand, ostrich tactics that I have to lay directly at the feet of my national democratic party. It is high time we quit hiding and took a stand. It is high time that the conservatives in the democratic party take action to reclaim our party.

The choice we have this year is the most clearly defined for decades. We must decide whether to cast our ballot for a president who will clearly take action to remove the terrorist threat, or a president who has stated repeatedly that he will seek approval of the United Nations before taking any action. Will you vote for a defender of freedom or an appeaser of terrorists.

Let's begin taking personal responsibility for what happens, it is high time we quit trying to abdicate it and realize that we have to begin from this day forward, acting as conservatives, not as democrats or republicans, or libertarians, or any other political party affiliate. You can no longer depend on a political party to act in your best interests. Gone is the day when we could feel that Democrats were for the working class

Yellow Dogs and Fruit Flies

and Republicans are for the Rich. Forget whether an individual has an "R" or a "D" in front of their names on the ballot.

Find out who is the most conservative and vote for them. If you are a democrat but the most conservative person on the ballot is a Republican or a Libertarian take a deep breath, hold your nose, and vote for the conservative. Only by voting **conservative consistently,** (and I mean on questions as well as candidates), can we regain control of the democratic party and turn our country around! If we must vote Republican in order to vote conservatively, then that may be the only way to effectively put our party back on the road to national prominence and make believers out of the radical Liberal element that now controls it. We gave control away, we can take it back! Refuse to listen to sound bite propaganda on the 6 O'Clock news, ask why, who, and how, and don't take no for an answer. Be an informed voter, or don't be a voter. You can no longer depend on the democratic party to do what is best for you.

About the Author

Rick Teal is Director of an Older Americans Act Senior Services program, and was an Infantry 1st Sergeant in the Oklahoma Army National Guard for 21 years. He also serves as president of the Oklahoma Association of Nutrition Project Directors. In these capacities, he has spent a great deal of the past thirty five years in some sort of government service, always striving to make our government work better for the people it serves, not the other way around.

He is a registered democrat, but has become increasingly dissatisfied with the liberal tilt to the left of his party over his lifetime. Rick is writing this book to help the Conservative Democrats of this nation take back their party, by explaining his thoughts on what has happened in Americans Politics during the past 40 years.

Printed in the United States
20867LVS00001B/214-225